Here Comes Everyone

Tony Bradman

Illustrated by Priscilla Lamont

CAMBRIDGE
UNIVERSITY PRESS

Here comes the morning,
here comes the sun,

2

here comes a black cat,

here comes . . .

everyone!

Here comes one boy,
here come two,

here comes a girl
with nice new shoes.

Here come two girls
with their mums,

here come two boys
sucking their thumbs.

Here come three girls,

here come four,

here come five boys . . .

and lots more!

Miss Miller's in the playground.
She's already there.

But who crept in the window?

Who's *that* on her chair?